THE PROMISE

D. B. PURKERSON ~ U.S.M.C.

By D. N. Purkerson

Dedicated to Mary Jo and her sons, Mike and Tony. There is much that could have been said here about quiet heroes, and the transforming power of a family's love.

IN MEMORY

In memory of the approximately 3,000,000 military and civilian deaths caused by the Korean War.

May the fruit of this conflict justify our mutual sacrifice.

****

CONTENTS

FORWARD

When my uncle, Donald B. Purkerson, passed away on April 27, 2008, I wrote this story for my family hoping to help them fully understand the challenges Don had overcome to be the lovable guy his friends, family, and community had come to hold in such high regard. Long before he shared his story with me late in his life, he had earned my deep respect for the way he conducted himself as a man.

Don had been among a group of United States Marines sent to Korea in a policing action for the United Nations in 1950. There, he was in several of the most significant battles in Marine Corps history, including the Inchon landing, the taking of Seoul, the firefight at Sudong, the battle of Chosin reservoir, and the passage through Hell Fire Valley. Those lucky enough to return became known as ***The Chosin Few***. Many suffered all their lives, not just from physical injuries, but from deep emotional scars left by the nightmare they endured.

Today we are starting to understand the effects of

trauma on soldiers returning from combat, but in 1950 the expectation was that soldiers should just come home and pick up where they left off. Often it just doesn't work out that way.

It was especially hard for the Korean veterans as opposed to the honored veterans of World War I and World War II. Primarily due to the press, the public lost interest, and Korea became an unpopular war. When the soldiers came home, the welcome they received was far from being the heartfelt thanks they deserved. It just wasn't right. The survivors had been through a kind of hell few people could ever understand. The fruit of their efforts serves us to this day, but few people ever fully realized the value of their sacrifice.

My mom's brother, Roy, was real quiet after he came home from the war. Friends and family didn't know how to help. They'd say, "He was a light-hearted kid 'till he came back from Korea." My friend Rose had a brother who returned home to spend the rest of his life sitting in his bedroom - he never spoke again. People just said he was "shell shocked." Rosie never married, staying to care for him until he died in his 80's. But somehow, my uncle Don's experience with his fellow Marines in Korea tempered into an unshakable faith in God, a lifetime pursuit of excellence in his conduct, and of encouraging the same in the people around him.

There have been so many authoritative books written about Korea; I confess I feel like a small guy stepping onto a field of giants. But I knew when Don passed away if I didn't tell his story, it would be gone.

I'm publishing this story because the men who fought in the Korean War are now in their 80s and 90s. It's a good time to share their stories and honor their sacrifice with the respect that is so long overdue. Also, I want to tell you about how Don found a way to go forward from a very hard time - my fondest hope is that you might find courage in his example.

This book is not Don Purkerson's life story. Don served in the United States Marine Corps from November 1949 to February 1953. This story focuses primarily on the extraordinary events of 1950, along with some relevant information. I did not choose to fluff this story up with drama - the facts alone are startling, grotesque, and heart-rending. I come away with solemn respect for what the men on both sides of this conflict endured, and with empathy for the suffering of the Korean civilians.

It should be said that Don would not wish to be remembered for his military service only, but rather as a faithful spouse, a loving father, a mentor to young people, and, above all, as a man of Faith. By the measure of many, Don would be called something loftier than "a good man," but not by his choice. It is for people like me, a scribe and part-time witness to the life of Donald B. Purkerson, to share what I know, so Men who served as well as he should not be forgotten. Please know I've done my best to honor their memory here with the Truth.

Sincerely, David N. Purkerson

(note: some names have been changed)

01) YOUTH

Donald B. Purkerson was born in May of 1931 in Eugene, Oregon. His parents were Alfreda Sarah and Chester Neil Purkerson. The family had a farm at Meadowview, just outside the small town of Coburg, near where the Purkerson family settled in 1854. One month before Don's sixth birthday, his father passed away, leaving Alfreda with six children: Kaye, Rex, Gale, Don, Dick, and Betty.

After Chester's death, Alfreda was approached with suggestions to break up the family. On her insistence, they stayed together. The small community looked on as she worked to see her children had love and a good home. She never remarried. All of the children of Alfreda Sarah Purkerson gained a lifelong respect for their mother, born from her example of Christian faith, honesty, and hard work. They *always* spoke of her with reverence. Once I asked Uncle Rex about this. He looked me in the eye and, in a most serious way, said, "*She gave her life for her children.*"

Don graduated from high school in 1949. By then, he had become good friends with the Harbert family of Coburg and worked on their farm outside of town. Harry and Marie Harbert had lost their son in World War II a few years earlier. It was very hard for them, but Mr. Harbert found a measure of comfort in Don's friendship. For Don, who lost his father so young, it was good to have an example of how a man should behave. He would later say Mr. Harbert was the closest thing he had to a father during that time. Don learned to drive and maintain trucks for Harry's brother Cecil a few months before entering the Marine Corps - a skill that would later serve him well in the military.

Don was 18 years old when he entered the U.S. Marine Corps on November 10, 1949. He attended boot camp at the San Diego Marine Recruit Depot in California and received further schooling at Camp Le June, North Carolina. After graduating, Don was assigned to duty at Camp Pendleton, CA.

Private Purkerson liked the rigors of Marine Corps life, and the code of conduct Marines live by. He was sharp, smart, and hard-working. Probably because of this and his experience driving trucks, Don was assigned to Major Warren Morris to be his aide. He was designated as a "motor pool mechanic," primarily acting as a driver for Morris, but also staying nearby to attend his orders.

Maj. Morris was the executive officer of the 3rd Battalion, 7th Marine Regiment, 1st Division at the time. He achieved the rank of major, having served with distinction during World War II. The Major was not a large man, but his bearing and manner inspired respect from those who served under him, including Private Purkerson. Fifty years later, Don would still remember the Major saying, "There are men who demand respect, and there are men who command respect."

02) HISTORICAL PERSPECTIVE

When World War II ended in 1945, the Korean peninsula was divided between Russia and the United States, but by 1949 there was a significant concern in the West about the sudden and violent spread of Communism related to the Russian/Chinese alliance. The Soviets tested their first atomic weapon in 1949. Chinese Chairman Mao Zedong publicly announced a plan for the global conquest of Communism. These events created an atmosphere of strong anti-Communist sentiments in the United States and were a threat democratic nations could not ignore.

By 1950, Communist North Korea became impatient to regain control of South Korea. China and Russia both felt it would be better if they could push the Americans out of Korea. In June of 1950, North Korea, trained and armed by Russia, invaded the South. The South Koreans were overwhelmed by the North Korean People's Army **(hereafter:**

NKPA). Within three days, the capital city of Seoul fell.

The United Nations then voted to intervene. This action was the first time in history American forces were sent to fight Communist forces. On July 1, 1950, American ground forces (U.S. Army) landed in South Korea. The U.S. Army believing the NKPA wasn't much of a threat, dispatched a modest force of 500 men to help the South Koreans. They suffered 125 casualties in the first battle against the North. Even the arrival of the Army's legendary 7th Cavalry could barely slow the NKPA's southward march - the harbors of Inchon and Wanson fell. The Communists were moving toward Pusan to push the American force off of the Korean peninsula literally. Along the way, they were excessively brutal to the South Korean civilians and military prisoners. On July 10th, the Marines discovered the bodies of several American soldiers executed by North Korean soldiers in Chonui, Korea. Major General Dean was captured, becoming the highest-ranking American prisoner of the Korean conflict.

Finally, on July 19, 1950, President Truman ordered the United States Marine Reserves to report for active duty.

Don

03) INCHON/SEOUL

*"It doesn't take long to become
a Veteran" D. B. Purkerson*

Since being assigned as an aide to Maj. Warren Morris, Private Purkerson had worked tirelessly. The Major found Don to be a very earnest, friendly young man - always eager for the next assignment. Though it is uncommon for an officer to become familiar with his driver, Morris especially liked Don, and when away from other soldiers, would often engage in more casual conversation.

One day in early August 1950, Maj. Morris unexpectedly gave Don a 72-hour pass to reward his weeks of hard work. He was insistent and even commented Don "should not show his face" around the base for a few days. Don went to San Diego to visit some of his high school buddies. Returning to Camp Pendleton 3 days later, he was shocked by the news: *Major Morris and the 3rd Battalion had shipped out to Korea, leaving him behind!* Don may not have understood at the time, but would later come to realize Maj. Morris was trying to spare him.

A dangerous plan for the retaking of South Korea had been set and would begin with a beach landing at Inchon. Losses in the initial landing were expected to be heavy, so many officers left newer recruits behind knowing they would come along in the second wave. Upon reassignment, Don found himself a part of the 1st Battalion, 7th Marine Regiment, 1st Division in a weapons company where he was trained to be an assistant rocket gunner. On September 1, 1950, they departed from San Diego, California, on the U.S.S. Bayfield bound for Korea.

On the way, they laid into Japan for one day of leave. Arriving in Korea, Don participated in securing Inchon from the North Koreans, followed by a march inland to take back the capital city, Seoul.

Before the Marines landed at Inchon, the United Nations force had been pushed clear to the southern tip of the Korean peninsula. The Inchon/Seoul action is now considered to be one of the most decisive victories in American military history. In one move, the 1st Marine Division landed and fought their way inland as the U.S. 8th Army with the South Korean Army troops pushed north out of Pusan. The result was to nearly destroy the overextended NKPA forces. Through the end of September, the Marines pushed northeast across the Han River to Seoul. When Don arrived in Korea, he weighed 165 lbs. By Seoul, he weighed about 135. (I once remarked to Don that Seoul wasn't far from Inchon. He said, "*It is if you're walking!*")

As an assistant rocket gunner, Don carried ammunition to assist the gunner in the use of a bazooka (portable rocket launcher). The gunner was a cocky young man named Chucky - tall with a face full of pimples and a nasty disposition. It seemed to Don like Chucky had been waiting his whole life for someone to bully around, and finally, Don showed up.

Chucky had been in the Corps about a month longer than Don, so he delighted in calling his assistant "Boot," an unflattering nickname given to recruits. When they were assigned to stand watch duty, the guy would fail to show, forcing Don to stand a double watch. He would take any occasion to taunt or harass Don, who patiently ignored his bad manners from the landing at Inchon through the taking of Seoul.

One day Chucky and Don were assigned to guard a road crossing some distance outside of town where reconnaissance expected a convoy of enemy vehicles and tanks to pass. Their assignment was to destroy the third or fourth tank to divide the convoy. They slept overnight in the bushes near the crossing, but no convoy passed. In the morning, the two received orders to return. As Don tried to hoist his pack, heavy with rockets, the gunner badgered him by grabbing the pack from behind. *Assistant Gunner Purkerson had had enough!* Don grabbed the rocket gunner by the pack straps on his chest and began spinning him around in a circle. At first, he dragged the guy around him, then gaining momentum the gunner's feet came clear off the ground, and he found himself being whirled around helplessly by his straps. At some point, Don just let him fly (with a pack full of live ammo) landing some distance away, sliding to a stop on his belly in the dirt. Words were exchanged, leaving no doubt about Don's plan for solving the problem if there was any further abuse. Chucky didn't bother Don again.

04) NORTH KOREA

Back in the U.S.A., a decision was now made that dramatically altered the events of the coming weeks. With the victory at Inchon/Seoul, the war had shifted in favor of the United Nations force. The North Korean People's Army (NKPA) was forced to return to their territory north of the 38th parallel. Everybody thought it would be a done deal by Thanksgiving, surely by Christmas. But, reluctantly, the United Nations, President Truman and the Joint Chiefs of Staff decided to back a plan by General MacArthur to continue pushing north to the Yalu River, the border of Manchuria (China). The plan was to push the remnants of the North Korean Army as far as possible without causing enough concern for China to enter the war. They did not know or possibly chose to ignore that China was already deeply concerned.

Don's unit was then ordered back to Inchon, where he had a fine turn of luck - he bumped into Maj. Morris. It seemed the Major was unhappy with his new driver, and seeing that Don had found his way to Korea, he arranged to have him reassigned to the 3rd Battalion, 7th Marines, 1st Division **(hereafter 3/7)**. At Inchon, 28,000 U.S. Marines, including the 1st Division of the USMC, were loaded on 71 Navy transport ships to sail around the Korean peninsula to take the port of Wonsan. They landed without resistance on October 26, 1950. The North Korean Army had retreated north.

At Wonsan, Don's unit (3/7) became part of a larger conglomerate force (mostly Marine 1st Division) known collectively as the "**X-Corps**" and received orders to follow the North Korean's retreat through the mountains north toward the Yalu River on the border of China. There was deep concern about extending the campaign into this location high in the mountains with only one road going in and out.

On Nov. 3, 1950, the division came under attack at night near the village of Sudong. It was the first time in the war Americans battled Chinese troops. On this day alone, the artillery battery within the 3/7 perimeter fired 1,431 rounds. In the four day battle, the Marines gained less than one mile at the cost of 300 casualties. Chinese losses were significantly higher. The Chinese prisoners reported as many as 50,000 enemy troops massed in the surrounding mountains. American intelligence still doubted the possibility of Chinese intervention. (Duh?)

As the X-Corps moved north into the mountains, they encountered an even more deadly threat. The weather turned bitter cold. Temperatures plunged to -30 degrees and below. It was the beginning of the coldest winter ever recorded on the Korean peninsula. Nature became the most ruthless enemy, not just to the soldiers, but civilians now being displaced by the conflict. Don later referred to it only as "The Cold" with a voice of lingering dread.

The wind was so strong Don struggled to stay on his feet. Wind chills below -120 degrees sent some men plunging into shock. Water froze in their canteens, fountain pens burst, and rifles jammed - the men had to move constantly to keep their blood moving. Their nostrils froze shut, having to be chipped open - faces were raw from wind and blowing snow that made it hard to see the enemy. Empty ration cans stuffed with explosives were sometimes needed to knock foxholes through the frozen ground. Don dreamed of being home if only for an hour, to remember the feeling of being safe and warm.

As a driver, one of Don's duties was to keep the Major's jeep in good running condition, no small task in sub-zero temperatures. All vehicles had to be kept running 24/7, or they would freeze up. The roads were steep, winding, one-laners, for the most part, covered with ice and snow. For Don, negotiating icy hairpin turns up and down the high mountain passes with a rock wall on one side, a cliff on the other, and an officer beside him could be a nervous thing. He had the advantage of driving instead of walking, but as Don would soon realize, the life expectancy for drivers wasn't good. An enemy that relied heavily on small caliber weapons quickly learned they could stop an entire convoy by shooting one driver. Killing a driver *with* an officer could earn one an extra ration of rice.

Knowing how much it meant to soldiers, a special effort was made to deliver mail regardless of how remote the location. In addition to letters from family and friends, mail call meant welcome gifts from home like cookies, warm socks, and stocking hats. One day during the cold, Maj. Morris received, along with his regular mail, a large box of powdered soap. The gift of powdered soap seemed curious to Don until the Major tore it open, producing a fifth of fine whiskey from home. He told Don to get his cup and poured them both a generous portion. It was November 23, and the troops celebrated Thanksgiving hoping for a speedy end to the war. Unfortunately, this was the last warm meal most of the men would have for some time.

05) ARRIVAL AT THE CHOSIN RESERVOIR / YUDAM-NI VILLAGE

T he Chinese People's Volunteer Army **(hereafter: CPVA)** was an immense fighting force that had recently been incited to intense feelings of nationalism by Mao Zedong's rise to power. Mao had gained virtual stardom by successfully pushing the Japanese from China. Now he turned his army to the task of driving Westerners from Asia. Secretly, throughout November 1950, the Chinese had carefully moved ten divisions into the mountains surrounding the advance of the X-Corps. Traveling by night, they had remained undetected by U.S. intelligence.

Because the Marine First Division was the most effective American fighting force, Chairman Mao Zedong committed over 120,000 Communist troops to isolate and destroy them. Their trap set, the enemy, silently waited as the 1st Division stretched its supply lines from the safety of Hungnam on the coast to over 70 miles north. There

Don's battalion arrived to set up temporary headquarters at the small village of Yudam-ni. The day was November 24. 1950.

That morning Don had felt hopeful when he read General MacArthur's communiqué to all troops saying peace was at hand. But when the 3rd Battalion arrived with advance units from the Marine 1st Division at the miserable frozen village, it wasn't much of a prize. Yudam-ni was high in the mountains on the Kaema Plateau at the western-most tip of a sizeable frozen reservoir that the Korean people call "Changjin" - we remember it as the Chosin Reservoir.

Blowing drifts of snow partially covered the broad khaki plain around the new headquarters, where the Marines spent the next three days concentrating their forces. Nearby hilltops were secured for the defense of the village and the main supply road south. Beyond the hills, five ridges extended from the valley floor up to the higher mountains north, west, and south of Yudam-ni. These would be secured next during the move toward the Yalu River.

The temperature was still below zero on November 27, when the Marines began to advance in stages west from the village. The plan was for 3/7 to hold the ridges straddling the route while other units passed through, but the 3rd Battalion encountered heavy machine gun and artillery fire from Chinese positions higher on Mt. Sakkat - casualties mounted - the wall of fire became so intense that every officer, except for one, was wounded.

When the news came about all the casualties Don and the Major must have been at the command post in Yudam-ni. I know that in the afternoon, Maj. Morris sent an ambulance forward from there, but it didn't return. Later they located the truck, but never found the drivers. Maj. Morris, with Don, must have chosen to accompany the two additional battalions being sent to reinforce 3/7 with a battery of field artillery (author's note: I was unable to verify this detail, but Don's story seemed to confirm they moved up to Mt. Sakkat. With the loss of officers it would make sense).

After the artillery arrived, the 3rd Battalion fought all afternoon to knock the bad guys off the ridge, but the Chinese fortified their positions too well. Other Marine units on the nearby ridges were facing similar problems. It became apparent the Chinese had heavily entrenched themselves north, west, and southwest of the Marine command post in Yudam-ni. By the end of the day, the Marines had suffered over 300 casualties, and 17 men were missing - they had advanced less than one mile.

Back at the command post, supplies and artillery ammunition were running low, so they decided to send all of their non-combat vehicles a few miles south to the 1st Marine Division's main perimeter at Hagaru. Unfortunately, they did not know the Chinese Army was quietly surrounding the southern supply route - the convoy was allowed to pass, but would never be able to return.

At dusk on the ridge, there was a lull in fighting except for light small arms fire. The day had been windy - when the sun went down the temperature was 20 below zero, causing weapons to become unreliable. 3/7 dug in far above the valley floor, preparing for a long cold night. Waiting quietly, knowing any minute could explode in chaos, left Don's joints stiff and his nerves raw. He was armed with only a pistol and carbine and hoped for a quiet night... no such luck.

06) FACING THE TIGER

"We've been looking for the enemy for several days now. We finally found them. We're surrounded. That simplifies our problem of finding these people and killing them."

Colonel Lewis B. Puller, commander of the 1st Marines

Several hours after dark, the quiet snapped when peculiar sounding bugles and whistles unleashed the battle of the Chosin Reservoir. Strange war cries and eerie chants gave the terrifying impression Death itself had come... and it had. Tens of thousands of soldiers from Red China's 9th Army poured down the frozen canyons onto the plain around Yudam-ni and points south along the main supply road. On the ridge, there was almost no time for Don and his buddies to respond before they were fully engaged. The Chinese charged from the darkness in human waves of hundreds after hundreds. The attack came so fast the enemy bayoneted some men before they could get out of their sleeping bags. The 3rd Battalion was pushed away from the top of the ridge but gathered their strength for another push to regain the lost ground.

They were nearly out of artillery rounds, which barely mattered now as they fought hand to hand with bayonets, small arms, and grenades. Finally, to avoid being destroyed to the last man, it was necessary to fall back to Yudam-ni. The gun crews loaded as many large field guns as they had rounds for, stuffed with any metal debris they could find. They aimed guns in the line of sight, directly into the face of the enemy. As the battalions retreated under pressure, Don looked back with horror as the howitzers were fired directly through the enemy with devastating results. The picture of destruction and slaughter he witnessed here still made Uncle Don emotional when he described it to me late in his life. Until that moment, I had never seen my uncle look vulnerable.

Back at headquarters in Yudam-ni, they learned that Chinese divisions had surrounded everyone - cutting the southern supply road they attacked south to Toktong Pass and Hagaru. It was a night of furious battle, with the constant threat of being overwhelmed. By morning, every U.S. battle group for miles along the supply road had become an island fighting to survive in a wash of enemy forces.

At first light, Don was with the Major as he surveyed their situation. The Major scanned with field glasses the khaki-colored plains punctuated with small hills around their headquarters and then handed them to his aide. Don later said, "I couldn't make sense of what I was seeing... it looked like the heads of wheat moving in the wind, an endless mass - *then I realized it was all Chinese soldiers!*"

Air support responded, dropping napalm into the sea of men. Don watched as enemy soldiers, delirious from cold, fell back to warm themselves on the flames of their comrades only to be cut down. The carnage was beyond the imagination of an 18-year-old farm kid from Oregon. Right then, Don decided his best chance at survival would be to stick by Maj. Morris, to obey his orders to the letter, and do his best to *make sure* the Major stayed alive.

Fighting continued without rest for two nights and two days. Machine gun emplacements had to be shifted to accommodate firing over mounds of enemy dead. The enemy reserved the most intense attacks for the night when they were less vulnerable to air attack. It was terrifying. At times the

Chinese succeeded in breaking through the command post perimeter but were so desperate from cold they couldn't organize a stand. When tracer fire ignited a nearby shack, hundreds of the enemy soldiers were killed as they swarmed in mass to get warm. Some Marine officers continued to lead despite being wounded 2 and 3 times. (Though Don never said so, it must have been a daunting task to keep the Major alive as he directed his troops in close combat. There was an extraordinary percentage of officers killed during the Chosin campaign. Credit to Don - he must have been a tough kid!)

By now, the medical area overflowed with wounded. Men's frozen fingers had to be broken to release their grip from their weapons - toes broke off when removing their boots. In the intense cold plasma wouldn't flow, and if left uncovered, wounds would freeze solid. For lack of space, corpsman bundled the wounded outside in sleeping bags covered with hay and tarps to help protect them from the sub-zero temperature.

The enemy acquired the high ground directly above headquarters, threatening to divide command from U.S. troops on the valley floor. The Marines countered by sending over 300 men from the 2nd Battalion to spend a terrible night defending the hill above - only 54 came down in one piece. Amazingly the defense held at Yudam-ni.

07) THE PROMISE

When the battle subsided, the 5th and 7th Marine regiments (including 3/7) found themselves isolated at Yudam-ni 14 miles from the 1st Marine Division's main perimeter at Hagaru. There was much reason for concern. Early on the morning of November 29, Maj. Morris led the 3rd Battalion in an attempt to open the route south. Almost immediately, they fell under heavy machine-gun fire. After hours of fighting, still unable to break through the heated resistance, it was necessary to fall back to Yudam-ni.

The night of November 29/30 fell silent, allowing the exhausted soldiers some measure of rest. Now came Don's darkest hour. Don had never been so tired, but he still couldn't sleep. Like everyone else, his mind was adding up the facts. They were utterly surrounded and outnumbered. The only route to safety was now a 70-mile gauntlet through canyons bristling with enemy entrenched on the high ground. Until this battle, most of the young recruits had never experienced a fight where the Marines did anything but overpower the enemy. Now, with the table turned, a dreadful feeling rose in Don's gut, realizing that most or all of them would probably die right here. It seemed like years since he'd kissed his mother good-bye, a boy eager to be on his own. Now he would give anything to be there safe and warm. How could he ever tell his mother the nightmares of this place? The family cut down trying to cross the field of fire to safety - the children frozen in a ditch where they sought shelter from the cold - enemy soldiers so desperate they warmed themselves on the burning bodies of their fellow soldiers, *"My God, who could ever understand this madness?"* As if in answer to the question, Don's worries were interrupted by a visitor, Lieutenant Chaplain Curtis Grayson.

Grayson was one of several chaplains attached to the 1st Marine Division. This night he was moving from man to man, no doubt exhausted himself, but hearing each Marine's concern. Chaplain Grayson was well-liked among the men, and Don was especially grateful for his company tonight.

Don was no stranger to prayer. He'd gone to church with his mom, sister, and brothers every Sunday, but tonight felt very different. On this night, death was so near as to create a vivid sense of how precious and fragile life is. As he and Grayson prayed together, every word seemed filled with vital importance, like some rending cry for help in the storm. Chaplain Grayson's prayer was so familiar. It brought his mother's simple words to mind. Alfreda would often say, "We live by the grace of God, and are sustained by our faith knowing he is always with us."

Tonight, her words about "living by *God's Grace*" and being "sustained by *Faith*" took on new meaning for Don. He saw that he had never been alone! *God was there* as a silent witness - and *God understands.* Don decided no army would choose the hour of his death - God would. Tonight Don would sleep, and if the morning came, he determined every step from here would be a step of faith. If he, or anyone, survived the Chosin Reservoir, it would only happen by the grace of God.

When Chaplain Grayson stood to leave, he paused several moments looking at Don and said, "Don, I want you to remember something: _We are the good guys. It's our job to set the example. And tonight, that example requires a good deal of courage and faith._" Before going out, Grayson looked back with a big smile,

"Get some sleep, Purkerson! Tomorrow's going to be a big day."

Later, in the dark, Don made a solemn promise to God, the same promise that every soldier makes when he's in a tight spot, "Just get me out of this one and I'll…"

08) THE CHOSIN FEW

The Chinese had made their entry into the field of battle at a terrible cost. They had expected to dispose of the entire Marine 1st Division in one sweep. Instead, after three days of intense fighting, the units at Yudam-ni still held their ground. The Marines were relieved to hear that, to the south, the defenses at Hagaru and Koto-ri had also survived. A single Marine battalion and the service troops from the vehicle convoy that left three days earlier from Yudam-ni managed the defense of Hagaru. Fox Company was pinned down near Toktong Pass but held its ground with the pure stubborn determination to not die.

U.S. Command had awakened to a different war. No longer was the enemy elusive or running. There was no longer any doubt as to China's concern about our advance toward the border. The U.N. force had taken nearly 2,000 casualties in three days, much of this due to the cold. U.S. Command decided they must regroup their forces or face the possibility of losing the entire X-Corps. Orders were issued on November 30 for troops around the Chosin reservoir to prepare for a move back to Hagaru as the first step toward safety at Hungnam far to the south.

By now, the number of casualties had reduced battalions (500 to 1200 Marines) down to the size of platoons (10 to 100 Marines). It was necessary to combine smaller units into composite battalions (Don was still in the 3/7). The men donned green bandanas made from parachute cloth and renamed themselves the "Damnation Brigade." They had been through a lot together.

You who have served will understand, adversity forges a bond between soldiers that transcends other relationships - stronger than fear, more profound than one's need to survive - a fierce loyalty, a brotherhood. By now, many good friends had given their lives to save their fellow soldiers, so it was with *great* reluctance; they made the painful decision they could not take the dead with them from Yudam-ni. The men conducted a field burial for their brothers before commencing the move to Hagaru. It is uncommon for a Marine to leave a comrade behind. The cold deepened. At regimental headquarters, they recorded -54 degrees, adding a layer of adversity that united these men forever. To this day, the World remembers them as *"The Chosin Few."*

09) THE BREAKOUT

Brigadier General Merrill Twining upon receiving news from his aide that the 1st Division was surrounded, "All I can say, young man, is that I'm damned sorry for those Chinamen."

I t is necessary to understand that moving military battalions requires extensive planning. The equipment needed to support this kind of operation requires bulldozers, tanks, artillery, and hundreds of vehicles to transport ammo, food, wounded, and dead. Also, air support must be coordinated by planners with each move. For military planners, regardless of the chaos of battle or how much pressure comes to bear, each movement is carefully considered - the field of conflict becomes a colossal chessboard. The United States Marines play chess _very_ well.

Remember that the night before the battle, most organic vehicles in Yudam-ni had been sent south to Hagaru, never able to return. For this reason, in Yudam-ni, they completed a rough airstrip evacuating some of the casualties until the area came under intense fire. All remaining vehicles they loaded with wounded men and supplies for the move - everyone "able" would have to walk (even Colonel Litzenburg commanding officer of the 7th Marines). This action might have been called a "retreat" had it not been for the circumstances - instead of moving away from the enemy, the UN forces would be advancing *through* the enemy to safety. They decided a more appropriate term should be used to describe the action - it would be called "the breakout."

During the breakout, close air support by Corsair fighter bombers would often be primary to survival. Gratefully, the day was clear on December 1st, allowing close support to the plans for "letting loose of the tiger's tail." Don would be in the thick of things: The plan called for three battalions (3/5, 1/7, 3/7) to take the point clearing the enemy from either side of the road to form a defensive line just south from Yudam-ni (same road they failed to clear yesterday, but there is no other choice). As the main column moved through, they would hold this line preventing the Chinese attack from behind. When the column moved south in the afternoon, heavy enemy fire from both sides of the road delayed them through another night of attacks.

During this night, most of the pressure came to bear at the rear where 3/5 and 3/7 continued to hold their line. After dark, a massive force of Chinese, division strength, raged against the defensive line until the Marines had to fall back from the hilltops. The desperate fight lasted into daybreak, reducing the two companies to a combined force of only 200 men, but still holding the 3.5-mile wide line to protect the rear of the column (that's about one man every hundred feet). At first light, Item Company to the southeast counted 342 dead Communist troops in their perimeter alone, but they had only 20 able-bodied men left. Don later recalled the morning cloud cover had prevented air support at a time so critical they might have been wiped out. He could hear the sound of corsairs circling above the deck, waiting for a break. Suddenly the clouds parted just enough. He said it was like the sky unzipped to allow the planes to pour through a narrow opening. Again Don found himself alive - another step forward.

10) A DESPERATE CHOICE

*"When times are good - reflect.
When times are hard - be
brave." Old Korean Proverb*

The combined column was now miles long and slowly climbing the frozen one-lane road toward 4000 ft. Toktong Pass. Here, many soldiers began reaching their limit, as the days of battle and subzero cold finally became too much. During periodic delays, numbers of troops were seen falling like dominoes unconscious in the snow, oblivious to enemy fire. Men had to be slapped and shaken to make them get up. The cold became a nightmare that wouldn't end. Some lost their minds and had to be restrained, later freezing to death from being immobilized. Many good Marines just fell over dead from cold and fatigue. Battalions were sent to run the ridges ahead of the formation. Their miraculous effort to clear the enemy from the path of the column was a testament to their courage and to human endurance earning these units the honored nicknames: "Darkhorse" and "Ridge Runners of Toktong Pass." To further slow the advance of Chinese divisions toward the column, the Marines burned Yudam-ni and destroyed the bridge there.

Here it should be noted there was a very different story unfolding as a by-product of the conflict. The civilians in North Korea had been forced to live under Communist rule for five years, since the end of World War II, and they didn't like it. They had fled their communities when the NKPA recently plundered their way through the area pursued by the Americans, and now their villages were facing invasion by the advancing Chinese Army. The Korean civilians were frightened of the returning NKPA soldiers, who had a reputation for ruthlessness. On their trail, the X-Corps often found civilians and our soldiers tied, mutilated, and shot. The local civilians were displaced when the U.S. Marines arrived at Yudan-ni, and other villages, but at least they were treated humanely. Now, faced with the cold and advancing Communist forces, most civilians made the desperate choice to follow the U.S. Marines departing from Yudam-ni.

As the column advanced, more and more civilians followed, placing themselves in great danger. Hundreds of families trudged through the snow, the sound of their suffering haunted Don and the other men. They tried to do the right thing, but attempts to allow families to travel within the convoy perimeter had to be stopped. Enemy troops began dressing as civilians to throw satchel charges under tanks and convoy vehicles. Out of necessity, the decision was made by command, that no refugees could be allowed close to the convoy. Continuously occupied with matters of personal survival, the men still took what pity they could on the plight of these poor innocents, even delivering several babies during the breakout.

Vehicles transporting the wounded reached full capacity. For more space, drivers strapped the dead on the outside to fenders, rooftops, even tied onto the barrels of the tanks. It was a hellish sight. Anyone able, also many wounded, walked the entire way. Vehicles that broke down or were damaged by enemy fire, the Marines would push over the edge to keep from becoming an obstacle on the precipitous one-lane mountain road.

The Chinese dynamited buildings, rocks, and debris ahead of the breakout to fill their path with obstacles. Sometimes trucks full of wounded slid off the road. The enemy took these slowdowns as a chance to ambush, so rescues had to be made under heavy fire. Every breakdown, every ambush, or even a driver killed by sniper would delay the entire column. It took 79 hours to travel 14 miles, but thankfully the last of the *Chosin Few* entered the Hagaru perimeter on December 3, including the remnants of the 3rd Battalion, 7th Marines. In true form, they snapped to attention, entering Hagaru with a proud cadence.

11) HAGARU

Hagaru (a.k.a Hagaru-ri) was a beehive of activity preparing for the move to the South. Here was a measure of safety where exhausted units could catch their breath. Don would occasionally cross paths with Chaplain Grayson going about his duties. It didn't take more than a friendly nod to know what each was thinking, "Another step! We're still here!" In the past few days, the population in Hagaru had swelled with the ranks of battered units making their way here from all points. Many were U.S. Army troops escaping from the eastern side of the Chosin reservoir, where Task Force Faith took tragic losses from several other divisions of the CPVA.

The Marine 1st Division's airstrip remained functional long enough to shuttle over 4,000 dead and wounded away from the battlefield (3150 U.S. Marines, 1,137 U.S. Army, and 25 British Royal Marines), and gratefully bringing 537 fresh troops to replace some of the casualties. The Chinese were quiet through the night of the 5th, taking time to build their strength for a final desperate push.

One of the best things about Hagaru was Tootsie Rolls! Rations beyond what the men required for the breakout needed to be eaten or destroyed. In addition to the mounds of pancakes and hot coffee, the abundant supply of Tootsie Rolls was a particular favorite among the guys starving for any nourishment to restore their strength. It seems the candy settled better than rations. Grinning soldiers went about their hurried duties with their cheeks bulging, an accumulation of frozen brown Tootsie dribbling down their chins. For the rest of his life, Tootsie Rolls would be a special favorite of Don. He usually had a supply with him to hand out to children.

East Hill was a prominent line of hilltops just outside Hagaru, overlooking the Marine compound and evacuation route. The enemy had successfully held this commanding position since November 29, allowing them to harass the military supply road south of Hagaru. To prevent this from becoming a problem to the column when it moved, Lieutenant Colonel Murray's 5th Marines would attack East Hill covering the column's breakout south toward Koto-ri. The Chinese were "dug in" well, so nobody was jumping at the chance for this duty. It's always tough to be the last ones out.

There was a silver fog in the early morning of December 6th, temporarily preventing air, artillery, and mortar support when they moved out. The 7th Marines took charge of security of the formation leading out from Hagaru with three battalions in front to clear either side of the military supply road. The 3rd Battalion (Don) would cover from behind. The head of the column was attacked just outside the village, delaying the progress until noon when the fog cleared enough for air support.

By now, harassing small arms fire from the enemy was so frequent it was all but ignored by the exhausted men of the *Chosin Few*. With all the equipment noise, it was hard to hear. Bullets routinely whizzed past throughout the day. Many drivers continued to be target by snipers. At one point, an enemy soldier leaped out from the roadside in front of the Major and Don strafing the jeep with an automatic weapon - gratefully, only the vehicle was wounded. In a later attack, a large ordinance struck the jeep's roof, blowing a big hole that went unnoticed by Don until later - again, no injuries.

An ambush two miles south delayed them until 3:00 p.m. By dusk, only 3 miles out from Hagaru, they were seeing masses of enemy troops on the ridge tops moving south. The Chinese were acting with a renewed sense of urgency, knowing Chairman Mao's plan to destroy the 1st Marine Division was in danger of failing. The X-Corps *must* keep moving - they decided to travel through this night despite expectations of increased enemy activity after nightfall.

In the evening, looking back toward Hagaru was said to look like the fiery top of a volcano as East Hill erupted with tracer fire, mortar, and phosphorus grenades. The last ones out of Hagaru, the 5th Marines, had their hands full as the 22-hour battle reached a new level of intensity.

12) HELL FIRE VALLEY

"Yea, though I walk through the
valley of the shadow of death..."
Holy Bible, Psalms 23

It was after midnight when the column arrived in the place they would later call "Hell Fire Valley." Here they discovered the unfortunate remains of Task Force Drysdale. A week earlier, Lieutenant Colonel Drysdale led a task force of his British Marines north intending to open this road ahead of the breakout. In Hell Fire Valley, they took 321 casualties and lost 75 vehicles. The grotesque remains of their ordeal littered the roadside with portent signs, and a dark mood passed over the 7th Marines. They passed slowly through the eerie confusion of scorched wreckage now manned only by the frozen dead in a blanket of fresh snow.

The Marines stopped at a sabotaged bridge - it had been quiet for too long. Don looked around at all the fresh footprints in the snow - a sudden feeling that something was coming. Suddenly, Major Morris ordered his men to the left flank for the defense of the column, and just as he gave the order, the enemy attacked. Almost immediately, a captain and first lieutenant were killed - a lieutenant colonel wounded. Tracer fire lit the canyon as mortar rounds thumped through the formation. One of the ambulances loaded with casualties was hit, causing further wounds - the men's cries for help might have gone unanswered in the chaos, but for Lieutenant Chaplain Grayson and his assistant Sergeant Marvin Carter. They ran through the confusion to locate the wounded men. As Chaplain Grayson performed last rites for a dying soldier, machine gun fire raked the vehicle striking him in the jaw. Also hit, Sergeant Carter threw himself over the Chaplain to protect him. Both men were killed by enemy gunfire.

The Commanding Officer of the 3rd Battalion, Lieutenant Colonel William F. Harris, near personal breakdown himself, led the counter-attack that managed to beat back the enemy. But sometime around 5:30 a.m., he disappeared into the field of battle and didn't return. Don's commanding officer, Executive Officer Major Warren Morris, assumed command of the 3rd Battalion.

By now, so many had given their lives, the situation so desperate, there was no way to stop and acknowledge this loss felt by so many. For the rest of his life,

Don recalled Chaplain Grayson with a solemn appreciation for the courage and faith he'd inspired on the darkest night.

The "division train", as it came to be called, was now eleven miles long. Nearly 10,000 military and tens of thousands of civilian refugees - the train was stretched clear back to Hagaru, where the long battle for East Hill subsided with dawn on December 7. Marine losses were minimal while estimated Chinese losses were 800 dead, and a record number of prisoners as more of the Chinese succumbed to the bitter cold. The Marines burned Hagaru and destroyed all the supplies and equipment they couldn't transport.

The Marines needed to destroy all bridges after being crossed by the division train. But as they wired explosives to the bridge south of Hagaru, a seemingly endless stream of refugees kept crowding to cross. The enemy was too close behind the column to allow more delay. Marine interpreters announced the danger over and over, but frantic to escape the CPVA advance, nobody would listen. With no other recourse, they destroyed the bridge. It was a terrible necessity. Approaching Koto-ri, there were further attacks on the center and rear of the column - X-Corps casualties were light while estimates of Chinese dead numbered from 500-800. The 7th Marines arrived at Koto-ri around dawn. They buried 117 dead and leveled the place as they left.

13) SURPRISE AT FUNCHILLIN

The next obstacle moving south was Funchillin Pass. The crossing of the pass was expected to be opposed by a strong attack from the Communists. Surveillance identified the presence of a significant build-up of enemy troops in the area. Beyond Funchillin Pass, the road would descend to a lower elevation. Don began to hope he might live to be warm again, but that seemed far away in the early morning of December 8th. A new storm was dropping 6" of fresh snow, reducing visibility to only a few feet and preventing the close air support that had become key to survival. A composite of several battalions (including 3/7) took the lead out of Koto-ri toward the pass.

Maj. Morris' 3rd Battalion was ordered to seize two hills a mile south of Koto-ri, but by 11 a.m., they were still fighting for the first hilltop. The division train couldn't move south from Koto-ri until the enemy was forced from the hills around the road. Colonel Litzenburg (Commanding Officer 7th Regiment) radioed Major Morris ordering him to commit the 3rd Battalion reserves if needed, but get the hills cleared. Morris explained he only had 130 men left, and they were all fighting.

Two additional units were sent forward to help. The X-Corps finally dislodged the enemy from the objectives by late afternoon. Marine casualties were considered light despite the loss of one lieutenant killed and two more officers wounded. During the delay, the Marines provided medical aid to the refugees and delivered two babies; unfortunately, civilians still could not be allowed to join the column. It was heartrending to hear their moans through the snowstorm as families huddled together without shelter.

The formation slowly inched its way toward a problem point on the military supply road where a high bridge at the Changjin Power Plant had been blown three times previously by the Chinese. The bridge was needed to enable the column to cross a deep gorge. Even in good repair, it was barely wide enough to allow larger vehicles to pass. This time the bridge would need to be replaced. To secure the site, the Marines needed to clear the Communist troops from several dominating terrain features.

As it turned out, the enemy had invested weeks in building bunkers connected by tunnels on the highest point. Command called it "Hill #1081", but the _hill_ was a _mountain_ overlooking the road at Funchillin Pass. A perfect vantage for an ambush.

To their relief, the Marines were told not to advance the column to the bridge site. It seemed Command had planned a little "surprise" for Hill #1081.

In the wee hours of this same day, December 8, from the other side of Funchillin Pass, help had been sent. Fresh Marine troops of the 1st Battalion/1st Marines (1/1) were ordered to move north out of Chinhung-ni at 2 a.m. toward the pass. Their orders were to kill anyone trying to stop the breakout through Funchillin Pass. These guys were spoiling for a fight, and eager to help the **Chosin Few**, whose plight was now on the front page of newspapers worldwide. In the silent pre-dawn hours, disguised in their snow-covered parkas, 1/1 used the cover of the storm to fall on the enemy catching them entirely by surprise as they boiled their dinner of rice. By nightfall, they had cleared all the bunkers short of the summit and settled in for some rest before an assault to the top the following morning.

December 9 dawned clear and cold for the routing of CPVA troops from the crest of Hill #1081. There would be no element of surprise this day as the remaining Chinese knew their time had come. Despite excellent support from air and artillery, it proved to be very costly. Of the 223 U.S. troops that left Chinhung-ni the previous morning in the snowstorm, only 111 were still able to fight by the time Hill #1081 was secure. They had annihilated an entire Chinese battalion of 530 men plus taken many prisoners.

Through much resistance from small arms fire, advance troops of the 7th Regiment managed to unite with soldiers from the south in the afternoon. Regiment 7 (includes 3/7) wasted no time moving in a company to secure the bridge site below. The enemy troops there were a pitiful lot, many frozen in their foxholes - those left alive were suffering badly from frostbite and gangrene. By rule, prisoners unable to walk were supplied with provisions and sheltered when possible, then left behind for the enemy to reclaim.

The logistics of transporting an entire bridge in sections from Japan to be airdropped in Koto-ri, carried 3.5 miles through the battlefield to be installed, then modified in place to accommodate everything from tanks to jeeps, was an excellent example of the popular credo: "Improvise, Adapt and Overcome." Able-bodied prisoners were directed to work on the bridge. They finished repairs before dark, and after some problems at first, the division train finally began moving through Funchillin Pass.

All night long, the weary procession filed slowly through the pass. British, Republic of Korea, and American military moved Communist prisoners and all manner of military equipment. Beleaguered Families of refugees pushed carts and herded livestock, newborn babies cried, all moving in the light of constant artillery flashes across the fresh, clean snow. News reporters had hopped planes sent to Koto-ri for evacuating the wounded. Against military wishes, they stayed with the division train and were photographing the scene. The confusion of unrelated sounds was said to merge into an eerie calm later mentioned by many witnesses.

14) WARM AGAIN

The safety of Hungnam was still 45 miles away, but for now, the Chinese and North Korean Armies were struggling. The truth is that once the Marine 1st Division was united back at Hagaru, there weren't enough soldiers in China to stand in their way. The CPVA pushed further south, making futile attempts to mount some final challenge. Caught in the open lowlands by machine guns, they continued across the field of fire until they were nearly spent. To many of the Chinese, the dishonor of returning home defeated would be worse than death. In honor of the Chinese Army, we should respect that, to a great extent, they were a volunteer army and truly believed in the cause they died for.

It seemed a lifetime since ten days ago, Don and all the other men had fought their way out of Yudam-ni, now just over 30 miles behind them. In terms of warfare, the United States Marine Corps is a highly respected fighting force bearing a long tradition of staying until the mission is complete. Despite their hardships, the men didn't like leaving the field of battle before pushing the enemy clear into China - it felt too much like defeat.

The **Chosin Few** would not understand until later that despite being victims of a colossal ambush, *they had decimated seven divisions of the Chinese Army (and elements of three others) so severely they never fought again during the Korean conflict. They brought over 100,000 Korean men, women, and children out with them. In the coming days, all civilians were cared for and transported to safety - the greatest rescue operation in U.S. Military history. A total of 17 Medals of Honor and 70 Navy Crosses were awarded to the men for bravery during the breakout from the Chosin Reservoir - the most ever for a single battle in U.S. military history. Russia and China - two budding "superpowers" - had viewed the United States of America as an irreverent young country with the dangerous idea of granting extraordinary rights to ordinary people. Ideals like Freedom, Liberty, Equality, and Justice are irreconcilable to dictators. The differences between us could easily have carried us into a third world war. This battle was a huge step toward creating the grudging respect that has shaped global politics to the present day.* But none of this was apparent to the men when they finally arrived in the safety of Hungnam.

The *Chosin Few* didn't arrive like a bunch of whipped dogs - they marched in as Marines. Reporters from all over the world were gathered to witness the event. They wanted soldiers to smile and wave for the folks back home, but most of the guys were suffering so badly from shock and frostbite they couldn't focus on such trivial things. The reporters described it as the "thousand-mile stare."

Maj. Morris had no time for the media. He focused his efforts on the welfare of his command. Don took him to report, and they gratefully learned that before their arrival, units had been assigned to prepare a place to receive them. The *Chosin Few* were given warm quarters with good beds, hot food, and showers.

When the Major finally dismissed Don for the night, it had been a mighty long day. Just sitting in a latrine and basking in a hot shower seemed like an impossible dream come true. As the water washed away the grime, for the first time, Don was able to assess his physical condition. His hands and feet ached from frostbite (and would for the rest of his life). There was a painful wound in his back he'd gotten from a fall during the breakout, now infected from lack of attention. "Not bad," he thought, "for a guy with a jeep full of holes!" He felt a certain sense of pride having delivered the Major in one piece, but then a thought occurred to Don that drained his pride and made him stop...he remembered whose grace got him here - the strength he gained from faith. God had answered Donald Purkerson's prayers.

15) GOING HOME

Fifty-eight years later, shortly after Don passed away from complications related to Parkinson's disease, I opened one of his books on the Korean War. Like a line from a poem, his bookmark fell from the last page. It said, "God keeps his promises!" That's the way Don always viewed his experience in Korea - like God had been faithful to him when he needed him most.

A question remained that bothered Don. The same one that haunts many War Veterans, "Why did I survive when so many good men died?" Being mindful of the promise he had made to God one dark night, he determined himself to **_be_** the answer to that question.

In time Don found that serving God, serving his country, and serving people brought him a measure of peace that many Veterans never find. Even when he struggled, he always chose to go forward with purpose.

Don was later transferred stateside, promoted to

Sergeant, and finished his tour of duty as a combat instructor. He met and married a beautiful young lady named Mary Jo. If angels exist, maybe they appear as friends or loved ones, arriving when we need them most. It was hard to adjust to being back home, but Mary was patient and kind. Together they created a loving, safe place for Don to slowly heal. They raised two boys together: Michael Paul and Anthony Gale - easily two of the best men I've met.

Mary Jo stayed with him all his life. It took time to put Korea behind him. Ultimately Don's faith and a loving family changed him - he became ripe and full. He tended a big garden of friends but especially loved to mentor young people - challenging them to be *great.* He'd say to the kids the same words he shared over the years with the agents serving with him in the Federal Bureau of Investigation, and his fellow officers when he served as a criminal investigator for the U.S. Forest Service, *"Remember, we are the good guys! It's up to us to set the example."*

I can't imagine how many lives he touched, but I'm certain many people will remember the man, who had been given something wonderful and did his best to say, "Thank You!" with his life.

16) DRINKING IN THE STORM

Mt. Hood, Oregon

You can tell it's raining hard when the drips from the eaves of our cabin turn into steady streams of water. I thought there might have been a noise from over by the neighbor's place tonight. They're not here in winter, so reluctantly, I left the protection of the porch to have a look around. It's always good to find nothing wrong.

On the way home, I stopped at the bottom of the driveway to look up and appreciate the warm lights from the house glowing through the cold woods. I thought how miserable it would be to spend an hour out here in the storm, or night, or a tour of duty. What if my home wasn't just up the driveway? What if home was half a world away like it is for a lot of our children turned soldiers tonight? What if I was afraid to go to sleep? Fearful of what might happen in the dark, in the storm.

The driveway had just about turned into a creek, the

rain was noisy on the tin roof of the shed, but maybe God heard this person's quiet prayer for the young women and men who volunteer their lives to assure our well being. They *trust* our leaders to be wise.

I prayed our leaders be worthy of that trust... or know how cold this night is.

Stopping beside the porch under the eave I filled my hand with rainwater and drank like it was my first taste - breathed it through my nose to smell the pure Pacific rain. I thought of my little boy drinking from my hand beside the river so long ago and felt deeply grateful for all we've been spared, and to all who weren't.

May God Bless and Keep You.

Don and Mary Jo ~ 2003

"If you want to be a hero
now is when you start,
live a life of courage
even when it's hard,
when no one else is looking
do the right thing anyway,
because heroes aren't born, Son,
heroes are made."

From the song *HEROES ARE MADE*
by T. Purkerson/S. Christensen/L. Qualsett
from the album *STILL AMAZED*
by HIGHLAND PARK
(available on iTunes)

Printed in Great Britain
by Amazon